The Hill of Sorrow
And
The Mountain of Joy

§

The Collected Poems
of Roland Verfaillie

Copyright © 2010 Purple Onion Press
All rights reserved

Published by Purple Onion press
Miami, Florida

Designed and produced by Sigmund Rich, Purple Onion Press
versessa@comcast.net

Other works by Roland Verfaillie published by
Purple Onion Press:
The Ashley Dancers
The Lie (screenplay)
the book of job(s)
the second book of job(s)

No part of this book may be reproduced, stored in a retrieval system, or transmitted in any form, by any means, including mechanical, electronic, recording, or otherwise, without written permission from the publisher.

Writers Guild of America, East, Inc.
Registration Number: I224158
Date Registered, January, 18,2011

Hill of Sorrow, Mountain of Joy
ISBN 978-0-9787085-3-5

Contents	Page
Introduction	5
The Hill of Sorrows and	7-10
The Mountain of Joy	
Traveler Series:	
Traveler	12-16
Traveler's Return	17-23
Traveler on the Road	25-29
The God's Work	31-36
Waiting for the Tiller Man	38
My Captive	39-40
Dune Crossing	41-42
Man Child	43-45
Ode to Florida!	46-47
Simple Wedding	48-49
Mae She Rest/In Peace	50-54
The Wedding Anniversary	55-79
("Till Death Do Us Part")	
Babble	80-94

A poet is an unhappy being whose heart is torn by secret sufferings, but whose lips are so strangely formed that when the sighs and the cries escape them, they sound like beautiful music... and then people crowd about the poet and say to him: "Sing for us soon again;" that is as much as to say, "May new sufferings torment your soul." ~Soren Kierkegaard

Introduction

I owe this work to the inspiration of Samuel McCord Crothers, the late 19th Century essayist. I was particularly encouraged by the seminal ideas espoused in his essay: "The Dame School of Experience (1920)." Here is an excerpt from the essay on which I felt compelled to act - "A prose writer gets tired of writing prose, and wants to be a poet. So he begins every line with a capital letter, and keeps on writing prose."

And this is what I've done. After years of writing prose in the form of the novel, I have ventured out, and taken up the quill, so to speak, to write poetry. Yes, I began every line with a capital letter, but I didn't just keep writing prose. Well, okay, sometimes I do. But I don't believe that the prose-poetry that results from this exercise in writing is anyone's best. It is good enough if it fleshes out the space between the lines of what passes for a paragraph or two of prose. It is only marginally successful if it communicates an important point-of-fact. It is better when it transcends the facts, and shines a light by which we can see what has been hidden behind them. Like the person blind since birth that *sees* colorful landscapes in non-localized places, I wish to develop such a transcendental state through which poetry may flourish.

I've shirked poetry. That is, writing it in the formal sense and having any aspiration of making it available to a critical public. After all, everyone's a poet, *and don't know it.* Right? Every other pre-teen writes poetry, because poetry is shorter and filled with more imagery and mystery than prose, making the reading and writing of poetry more interesting and fun. Around middle school age, kids will have learned to progress from menial, structured writing assignments to assignments requiring a bit of sophistication in their language as well as in their creativity. Most pre-teens and teens don't seem lacking in imagination, and emotion; two key ingredients for a batch of poetry. Such writing expression goes hand-in-hand with the sempeternal blathering of teens that they carry on with in their efforts to achieve self-discovery and to understand their relationships with others. This age group is no less challenged than an adult in constructing mysterious messages, images, and metaphors through which we all seek to make life meaningful. To see life in a way that gives substance to the ineffable. Those between middle school and high school age tend to write poetry about their personal lives. About school, home life, future dreams, schoolgirl and schoolboy crushes, original stories, nature, philosophy, and everything else that runs through the mind of a preteen. This is the same busy traffic that runs through the daily lives of kids of all ages.

I am well beyond my teen years. In fact, I am beyond my generative years. I now compensate by cataloguing the treasures I find today; not of what I prospected in the past. The years I've lived upon on this earth, haven't made me wise, and they haven't made me a poet. I know it has to do with being awake and attentive to the beauty present in the moment. It is incumbent upon us to be open to discovering new ways to see and experience this life. I hope to transcend the conditioning that can make our lives seem mundane, cataract our vision and mute the sounds of nature. I never want to see tomorrow's rainbow, as just another rain shower that has passed in anticipation of another sunny day. I want someone to ask, "Tell me how a rainbow's made, and why it went away." I hope to have the rainbow make that transcendental journey to the page, and enable me to answer with a poem.

Roland Verfaillie

Hill of Sorrow
Mountain of Joy

I see the signal fires on the open range.
They are not burning to guide the lost.
They pull in those who rejoice,
In being found,
To be drawn to the fire like insects,
On a moonless desert night,
Offered light and warmth,
Bright enough to blind the night vision,
Of hunting owls,
Hot enough to raise the flames,
Like fiery tongues of dragons,
Licking the dark matter,
And devouring the universe.
Scant fuel is wings and spindle legs,
Better is the flesh and bone,
Of the hapless wayfarer,
More substantial to feed the Eternal Flame,
Used to keep vigil at the grave.

They come in endless procession,
Seeking asylum in the warmth,
Of false shelter in hostile camps,
Dispersed along the plain.

I recede into the shelter of shadows,
Where seclusion is the safe companion.
From here I can survey the wilderness,
And estimate my worth in the absence of things.
And where I can measure the distance,
To *Tierra del Fuego,*
Not in the distance between waypoints,
Or in the speed of the horsepower,
But rather in the echoes of a heartbeat,
And the throbbing murmur repeated,
In the rushing rivers of bloods.
For any other measure that collapses distance,
Would surely hasten my journey's end….to
Where the camp fires burn.

I stand on the jagged ridge,
And gaze into the smoke-black gauze of night,
And there comes a darkening of these regions,
Advancing like ink from the glands of Octopi,
Muddying clear waters,
Spreading in detonations of black velvet…Unfolding.
And there appear a million pinholes,
That pierces the dark fabric of the night sky,
To let the light of tomorrow bleed through,
In stark profusion against the curtain of the night.

The morning sun boils from the horizon,
Like magma clotting the wound,
Of a damaged earth,
Rent open by hydraulic pressures,
Of shifting plates agitated by the misery,
Of buried corpses,
Plowed under daily by disease and war,
What, but a cry and a shudder,
From the heavens can be heard.

I descend to the plain,
Where the signal fires burned,
And stand in the Polybius Square,
Of distorted meaning, writ shorthand,
By a menace that sought to deceive the needy,
The naked, the hungry and the lost.
What I did see…
Will crush the hopes of the timid,
And destroy the fragile spirit…

There in perpetuity are the dancers,
Ringed around the cooling embers,
Fastened to a scorched earth amidst calcified bones,
Androgynous silhouettes fused in tar and ash,
Stick figures grinning and freeze-framed,
Like the rusted sculpture,
Posing above the gates of concentration camps.

They are grounded,
Welded to a desert floor,
That shimmers and glistens like a cruel mirage,
In a nation of parched wilderness.

Fused sand becomes molten glass,
In the aftermath of hell's wrath,
Warned by the signal fires,
That burned on the open range.

Traveler Series

"Our battered suitcases were piled on the sidewalk again; we had longer ways to go. But no matter, the road is life." Jack Kerouac

Traveler

He carries with him the necessities of travel
For his journeys take him to far away places
To foreign countries ,
To live among strangers
And walk in solitary contemplation,
Along sunlit avenues.

His hearing attunes to the strident tongues
Of the old world ,
And seeks greater comfort still ,
In the mellifluent language,
Of night crickets, spring cicadas and song birds.

He has explored the wild mountain passes,
And followed the dry river bed
To the purple lupine meadows,
He has run through fields of rye,
And scaled the alpine slopes collecting wildflowers.

He has chased the elusive Mercator of the sun ,
To catch its golden promise.
And he has failed to catch the prize,
He has given up the search .

He lays down his rucksack
To rest in the shade of the bosky woods,
He has built his fire against the dark , cold night,
And bedded with his faithful and devoted ...
Desolation Angel.

Desolation Angel

Traveler, you follow the path of the dead,
For you seek beauty in far away lands,
Among strangers whose language you can not comprehend,
Traveler, you discover landscapes,
Verdant, fertile and lush.

Traveler , you are a solitary one,
You take no companion other than me,
To share the beauty ,
Of your majestic mountains, and secret glades,
I am not a living soul ,
Whose beating heart you can hear,
I have no love to give you.
Though you embrace me by your fire,
I can not give you warmth.

Empty the burden that you carry,
For you think its on you back ,
In that heavy load you carry,
That you call the necessities of travel.

I will give them voices you can hear,
In a language you can understand ...
If you will listen.

Necessities of Travel

Stone...
" I am the stone that guards your heart."

Role away the stone from my heart,
Pick up the fragments,
And put them back together with,
Sand, silt, and clay,
Roll away the stone,
Roll away the stone from my heart.

Iron Bars...
"I am the iron bars that keep you safe,
I keep out everyone - even those who will not hurt you."

Remove the iron bars from my lonely heart,
Let her in who loves me,
Even though it does not feel safe,
Pick up the iron bars,
And put them back together with,
Taffeta, silk, and lace
Remove the iron bars ,
Remove the iron bars from my lonely heart.

She

He meets her on his descent,
From that steep pass he feared to climb,
Because his burden weighed him down,
And winded him, and made him tremble ,
At the fearful height,
And rarefied atmosphere.

She stands at the head waters of a great river,
Her gaze makes him afraid,
For her beauty is a blinding light,
And her radiance pierces every atom of him.

They are the fragments of glassine crystal,
Healing and powerful ,
The not so gentle balm ,
That starts a stone cold heart.

Oh, Lady

Roll away the stone from my heart,
Pick up the fragments,
And put them back together with,
Sand, silt, and clay,
Roll away the stone from my heart.

Traveler

I will not,
Though I will help you.

She is still,
She does not move,
The land …it serves her,
And the world …speaks through her,
In words that I can hear,
And it is the poem of a lover.

She is beauty quintessential,
Unaffected by time,
And earths rough turnings,
She embodies the fire of the sun,
And the earth's hot core.

Her golden hair is pampered by the breeze,
It attracts the Mercator of the sun,
And guides its beams of sunshine,
To spread across the vast cascades.

She stands in the posture of the goddess,
Though she is not,
Her countenance is royal,
With Red lotus at her feet,
And woven flowers in her hair.

I am glad that she is flesh and blood ,
And the beating of her heart,
Keeps rhythm with mine own...

And she is willing to lay beside me,
When the nights are cold,
And light the dark,
When I am lost...
I do not feel alone.

Remove the iron bars from my lonely heart,
Let her in who loves me,
Even though it does not feel safe,
Pick up the iron bars,
And put them back together with,
Taffeta, silk, and lace.
Remove the iron bars ,
Remove the iron bars from my lonely heart.

I will.

Traveler's Return

Traveler

I am home ,
That place where I had left my heart,
For: "Home is where the heart is."
Though mine is safely hidden ,
Among my collections,
Of non numinous things ,
Like that little alien ,
Hidden in the menagerie ,
of children's playthings.,
Once valued, now forgotten.,
Yet kept in solemn perpetuity ,
Like a shrine to some lost child.

Home

Traveler you are back,
Back to claim your place ,
You say (though we do not),
Among the stuffed and lifeless artifacts,
That you abandoned long ago,
Before your journeys took you from us?

Heart and hearth have suffered in your absence ,
No light, no fire, no warmth in this old house,
For you have doused them all in the waters ,
Of the rainy season ,
And the cold winds,
Left in the wake of your departure.

Traveler, do not be fooled,
For this is no Outermost House ,
For wayward. men lost among the dunes,
Cast ashore from a foundering bark ,
Wrecked upon the unforgiving shoals ...
You can not take comfort here!

Traveler

I am proud and will not beg your favor,
I will not ask for shelter,
Or a fortnights rest upon a hard pallet,
I will not grovel at your door ,
Hungry and cold , and braced against the wind,
For I am accustomed to these conditions.

I will not take all the blame upon myself,
For you also neglected to light the fire,
You did not bar the door against the elements,
And you lain in the cold and the dark,
And muttered to shadows,
Mistaking them for me .

We are not one, but are the same,
We are accustomed to empty dwellings,
Inhabited by spirits of the dead .
The zeitgeist of our olden lives,
Has made of restless ,
And will give us courage…

When the shadows disappear.

House

Traveler, you are so indestructible,
And I envy your resilience,
When mine has failed me,
And made me hate you.
Now, you know I mock you ,
With my words.

I am just an empty house,
Whose echoes tell me ,
What my heart would teach me,
If it could speak again ,
Would the warmth of the hearth ,
Restore the beating in my breast...
And fan the embers into flame.

Traveler, you are clever,
And you beguile me with your charm.
You were my lover,
You ignited mighty passions in me,
And gave me purpose through desire.
Now, you know I mock you ,
With my words.

Traveler

House, you know I'll miss the spirits ,
You hold within each room,
And every recess, nock and cranny of you,
For I do not easily forget the safety and the shelter,
You once provided me without condition,
When I came home to rest...

I do not mock you with my words.

House

Do not enter this old house,
And do not lay your rucksack down,
Although you tell me it is light,
And will not crowd my spaces,
With your necessities of travel ,
Your visit will be brief ...

I will surly make it so.

Traveler

House, I will go,
And take with me ,
The exigencies of starting over.
I take what is mine,
The rest is yours to keep ,
Or to burn in the hearth ,
To heat your fury,
And defend against the Nor' East storms.
I must replace the tattered shoes,
My soles worn thin,
By walking endless trails ,
To reach some bare summit ,
Or to lose myself,
In the labyrinthine canyons ,
Of a parched desert.

I take with me a lock ,
Of silky, raven hair,
That I have kept these years,
Shorn in the earnest promise,
Of the pagan vows.,
My former lover swore ,
Upon our sacred union.

House, I do vouchsafe...
I will not work some magic ,
On this talisman ,
Of an ancient promise, violated.
I take it for it is light to carry,
Yet heavy on my heart...

It is my fine cross to bear.

Traveler

Leave the window open when I go,
Let the sun...shine in!
Chase the shadows from the corners ,
Watch the dust of ages ,
Dance in the tangled embrace ,
Of golden shafts of sunshine.

I pray the season changes soon,
And the poplars, elms and birches,
That I passed along the way,
Rejoice in their renewal .
For when I passed them,
They were barren ,
Anchored in permafrost,
And frozen to their core.

Traveler

I choose my path,
And it is to the East,
To meet the rising sun.
To see the early buds of Spring,
Upon the trees,
And I am overcome …

By the perfumed scent,
That fills the air,
That is the breath ,
And blood,
And sweat ,
Of mother earth…

She, who is my one true lover,
A lasting love,
That's mine forever.

House

Good -bye

"Your true traveler finds boredom rather agreeable than painful. It is the symbol of his liberty-his excessive freedom. He accepts his boredom, when it comes, not merely philosophically, but almost with pleasure." Aldous Huxley

Traveler On the Road…

I embrace the world as I imagine ,
It once was…
Elegiac, vast and mysterious,
Informed by tales and legends,
Crafted by adventurers, and story tellers,
Men possessing great gifts of artifice and fiction,
Whose journeys sometimes ended in disaster…
When their hope was for safe passage,
And a share of untold riches.

I have steered clear of dangerous passages,
And roads controlled by highwaymen,
I have avoided places spoiled by the Soldiers of Fortune,
And the ruthless Captains of Industry,
Whose ravages upon the land,
Have left it barren like a baleful woman,
Grieving for her unborn child.

My book of travels is soft bound,
In the Oral Tradition,
Guarded by a mortal librarian,
Whose memories are fading slowly and surely,
As the wing beats of a dying butterfly ,
Impaled upon a thorny branch,
And passing without consciousness of dying.

Like this metamorphosis,...
From the fullness of experience,
To the threadbare legacy,
That gives no inheritance to our progeny,
It will not last without sharing with another,
I am told,
And will disappear in the glassy lune ,
Of a lifeless pair of eyes.

I am as bound for extinction,
As the creatures of the Rain Forests,
And the histories of lost civilizations.

For in this short life,
Upon a world so fixed in the timeless universe,
Must I commit to another,
An account of my O'significant life,
(No less important than the butterfly's),
And itemize the precious things,
That I have garnered along the way...
Or someday fail to recollect?

Yes.

So, I shared with my kindred spirit
The beauty I have found,
In the hidden meadows of my soul,
And the secret valleys of my deepest thoughts.
I have taken him to the mountain hideaway,
Where my ancestors dwell in the solid granite,
Beneath the snow capped peaks,
And whose wisdom is passed on to me,
In the dull whisper of falling snow,
And when I fail to understand,
On the tremolo of mountain wind storms.
This before my witness,
Should you doubt the truth of what I say.

I am happy for more time upon this earth,
To travel farther,
To comb the Hemispheres,
And wrap myself around the Prime Meridian.
I will plot a course that rides roughshod along the equator,
And seek comfort from the heat of the summer sun,
In the Tropics of Cancer and Capricorn.

I will spare myself the extremes,
And not take rest,
In the lifeless Polar Regions,
Of the world...
Where icy rivers,
Scar the Continental ice sheets,
Like spider veins,
Snaking the weary legs of age'd walkers...

I seek a fit companion though,
Who will weather the arduous journey,
And share with me the sweet reward,
Of basking in salubrious climes,
And lie down with me,
In the may flower meadows.

I ask that she will do the same,
When the embers of the campfire,
Grow cold,
And make us wretched,
In the dampness and desuetude,
Of nature's poverty.

We will be witnesses,
Before the fact, and after,
And hold the misfortunes,
We may suffer,
Through the ravages,
Of winter blizzards, summer floods,
And autumn famines…

To be the wrath,
Of nature's fickle mood,
And not our own…

For we have no power,
Over any majesty or calamity…
Other than our own.

The poem... is a little myth of man's capacity of making life meaningful. And in the end, the poem is not a thing we see - it is, rather, a light by which we may see - and what we see is life. ~Robert Penn Warren, *Saturday Review*, 22 March 1958

The Gods' Work

Gods :
Listen…
And act upon the works,
That I would have you do,
For you are mine own creation,
Born in the precuneus,
Of divine gray matter.

Gods…
I give you sacred names,
And I worship you in the temples of Tibet,
And genuflect before your images,
In the churches, mosques and synagogues,
Of the Western theocracies.
I summon the awesome powers of the Odic force,
And for all my prayers,
I am granted only milliamps,
Of feeble power,
To light a torch,
Whose light is unsubstantial…
Ephemeral as a spark,
Ignited by flint & steel,
When suddenly introduced…
The barest flicker of hope,
Against the dark matter,
Of the universe.

I have borrowed heaven's energies,
And owe a debt,
That I will repay,
Beyond my dreamless sleep,
Or when all vanishes,
In the violence,
Of the Kaliyuga.

I am deep in debt,
For otherwise,
I would be nothing more,
Than:
Dull reasoning,
And a barely beating heart,
Buried deep,
In the hollow cavern,
Of my breast.

That is not all that I am,
For I am capable of wondrous things,
Like the miracle,
Of Love,
And the creation,
Of another life.
More perfect,
Than my own.

I rule this vast, great empire,
Criss-crossed,
With endless thoroughfares,
Of writhing ganglia,
And I possess one-hundred billion neurons,
That I command,
To do my will,
And initiate my pleasure.

These are the gods,
 Who will obey me,
When I tell them:
Recreate the world,
Fulfill my wishes,
And design the world,
According to my plan,

Shiva:
Draw the curtains tight,
Blow out the candles,
And turn off the lights,
And let me love again,
And imagine my old lover,
Beautiful and young,
The story-lines of age,
Writ deep upon her face ,
And the tilted axis of her posture,

Disappearing…
In a magic act,
Performed in darkness .

Let us greet one another…
And emerge from the liquid shadows,
Of the ebony void,
To coalesce as one,
In evanescent splendor,
Like black gold,
Dappled with indigo,
And with a fire burning redly,
When we touch.

Mila-Raspa:
Work this miracle for me,
And teach me words,
That I might sing,
To the music,
Of your hundred-thousand songs.
I will sit at the foot,
Of the lotus asana,
And be your eager student.
This I would command you,
If I did not fear the more,
The begging bowl,
You hold in your left hand,

For I am penniless of virtue,
And in debt beyond,
The dream time of eternity.

You cup your hand to your right ear,
Listening to the echoes of nature,
Pretending:
That the mysteries of life,
Are revealed in the titter of birds,
And the tympani of distant thunder.
You reply in song,
In imitation of their speech,
But, unlike me…
You fail to understand…
It's only idle chatter.

Mila-Raspa:
Leave well enough alone.
And do not beg from me,
For I have nothing more to give.
And do not teach me the words,
To your hundred-thousand songs,
In the Karaoke for the masses.
Convert me if you'd like,
To your religion,
Where giving is its own reward,
And pays back generously,
Measure for measure.

I will give my lover,
The balm of gentle goodness,
That I have learned to give...
I will leave the lights off,
And embrace her ...
Like Vaj ra va ra hi ,
And tangle,
In the black silk sheets,
In the Sa haj pleasures,
Of our lust.

I have no shame ,
For what I pray,
For I command it,
From the reptilian god,
That made me from the mud,
For I am what the gods have made,
And I re-create them,
From the parts of me...
That can.

Sorrow and Joy Series

Poetry is the art of substantiating shadows. ~Edmund Burke

Waiting for the Tiller Man

I descend into the pool of lividity,
The particles of me in detritus rest,
Well oiled in life,
Now a stain on a satin sheet,
Rust of earthly coil,
Dust brown as tannin,
Pungent as low tide,
Congested with annelid slime,
In death.

My soul is spun in gossamer,
Afloat in limbic preconscious time,
Busy thoroughfare of primitive impulse,
A flickering beacon for the tiller man,
On a collision course with the rocky shoals,

On impact souls disintegrate,
Freed from the ever-present,
Pain of remembrance,
And the guilt of unfulfilled dreams,
Repeated in death's sleep,
And awakened in infant possibilities.

My Captive

Dreamy butterfly hovers,
'Round the honeysuckle bush,
How odd, it doesn't flutter very far,
Easy to catch and make my prisoner,
Now lighted on a dried twig,
Inside a soured mason jar,
Not believing, I imagine,
In the glass partition.
§
Now perceiving a winnowing,
Out-of-focus world beyond,
And muted human language.
§
Now living on pickled air,
Myopic, and senses impaired.

Ole butterfly's wings open and close,
Fanning tepid air,
In one-two scissor motion.

Once, butterfly spun a cocoon,
And slipped into worm skin,
In preparation for the sleep,
That brings the dream of… change,
Is this how change begins?

Light of day pierces glass,
And lets in streaming rainbow colors,
While the fingers of the captor,
Look like daddy longlegs,
As a funhouse face,
Looms grotesquely and slightly comical,
But butterfly feels safe,
In its private glass bubble,
That keeps out birds and bumble bees,
Avoiding all kinds of trouble.

Oh, butterfly, you're fading fast,
More merciful would be the killing jar,
Glass world keeps out,
The things that count,
Caressed only by the hand,
That holds the jar,
And leaves a greasy print,
For failing eyes to read,
Like cuneiform writing.
On a cave wall.

Butterfly is dying...
Denied what's real,
And fed on crumbs and emptiness.
Missed is the honeysuckle bush,
Forgotten is the garden.

Dune Crossing

Dunes of sugar sand stretch for miles,
Mother earth on her back,
Laid back, fertile, voluptuous,
Her mounds of fine silica soft and warm,
As she spreads wide to the Province Lands,
Wet in the shallows of Pilgrim Lake,
The wind rippled sand spits,
Spawned by retreating tides,
Lay bare the windward shore.

She wades in the shallows,
Of Highland Light,
In need of a razor clam pedicure,
Her knotted mane of silken sea oats,
Is combed by the breezes,
Of the Truro headlands.

I see only beauty in her lazy repose,
And I whisper, "Sweet Ishtar,"
My words carried by a gentle wind,
That curls and caresses,
While the sweet scent,
Of her rosehip perfume,
Excites my senses.

Today I will mount her,
Striding to the rhythm,
Of the pounding of my heart,
And oh so slowly crawl,
To reach her summit,
And in the gloaming before the dark,
I will breach her crimson cliffs,
 Reflecting the reddening passion,
Of a resplendent sunset,
Bleeding into night,
And in the mercurial black,
Of the *Devil's Top Hat*,
I will succumb to the pleasure,
Of my little death,
And thrill to the rush,
Of my sudden resurrection,
To lie there in the half sleep,
And the twilight dreaming,
That a thousand poppies bring.

Man Child

The fog of memory has lifted from my eyes,
For there my father stands,
And I can read like ancient petro glyphs,
His character etched indelibly,
In a wind burned face,
Resembling map lines and sea serpents,
Sketched on old parchment,
Suspended in time,
Like George Washington staring down at me,
From Mount Rushmore,
And the Black Hills,
Telling their stories all around.

The dust of memory has emptied from my ears,
For I can hear my father's story,
In the music of the spheres,
And in the eerie noise of silence,
And my hearing sense is tuned,
To the pitch of a tuning fork.
For I am a diving water witch,
Possessed with the knowledge,
That a raging current flows,
Beneath the placid surface,
Of fathomless, black waters.

The chains of memory are lifted from my feet,
For once upon a time,
The tenebrous instincts of childhood,
Kept me from entering the shadows,
Where rejection waited,
And I cowered in the corner...forever nearly,
Waiting for the sun to rise,
On the promise of another day,
Frightened though I was,
I ventured into daylight,
(Fevered eyes peering through simian fingers),
And walked stiffly to embrace my father,
Coming down the road.

The pillory of memory is lifted from my hands,
For fathers and sons fear the concupiscence,
Lurking in a hug,
And panic in the feminine imprecations,
Of their love,
Perhaps a death beds kiss,
On a withered cheek,
Or a handshake firm and manly,
But I am needy, green and hulking,
Always hoping,
And after raging, frozen motion,
Of feinted action broken...reaching,
I hold my father...we are rocking.

The gag of memory is removed from my mouth,
For once there was a time,
When I heard… nothing,
Yet listened attentively,
For the angry echo,
Of a word shouted to the stony cliffs,
And barren ramparts – FATHER!,
Dumb, my crie du chat monologue,
The language of troubled infants and fools…

Though now…
We speak the wireless words,
Of understanding,
And comprehend,
The multi-lingual languages,
Of the heart.

The stone of memory …
Is lifted from my heart.

Ode to Florida

Florida! A feverish state of mind,
Ellis Island of my time,
Her beaches pregnant with each rising tide,
Delivers when her waters break,
A population boon,
Many of whom, Chrome Detention Center
Will accommodate.

Florida! Tropical, far from ice,
Compared to Newark and the Bronx,
It's paradise...
Traffic jams, macadam, condos, lotto land,
Enclave of damn Yankee towns,
Carpet Baggers selling houses built on,
Everglades muck, and dredged up sand.

Florida! Home of the immigrants, the Mets,
And the Marlins,
And also the well fed, financially fixed,
And the starving,
The sounds from the melting pot ...
Bitching, complaining in an unintelligible polyglot.

Florida! "It's a Small World After All,"
Where worshipers of the Mouse
Make Orlando their Mecca,
Just to hear: "Hello Boys and Girls,"
In a phony falsetto,
Where suddenly gone is the ghetto,
And also the polyglot,
From Magic Kingdom to Epcot,
Not bothered by have-nots,
Reminds me that what's important,
Is keeping what I've got.

Florida of Old! I sure do miss you,
Pristine shores, and tacky souvenir,
And shell shops,
Nehi in bottles and surf shops,
Making fun of the snowbirds,
Wearing socks with their flip-flops,
Gone are the rhythms,
Of beach party bongos,
Replaced by the staccato,
Of Mac 10s and Glocks.

Simple Wedding

My eyes behold the beauty of her face,
Features painted on a flawless canvas,
Accented in gentleness and grace,
Framed in the symmetry of Belgian lace.

She is bathed in a prism,
Of rainbow iridescence,
Poured through liquid amber,
In fractal splendor,
Following a summer rain.

Her raiment is plain,
Not opulent,
Not wove from gold,
And hemmed in precious rubies.

She is beauty quintessential,
No need for man's additions,
To finish her perfection,

Her cerement though plain,
And worn by common peasants,
Is spun from flaxen fiber,
And trimmed in purple thistle,
She needs no more than this...
In this she is complete.

She stands beneath the arches,
Of a pagan altar,
Built upon a power place,
Deep in the forest primeval,
Betrothed to a lover,
Related to the faun.

The cry of the hawk,
And the ballad of the minstrel,
Announce the final moment,
When vows like sacred pacts do seal,
Love's lasting promise,
And its binding commitment.

Her lips draw near,
And meeting mine,
Precipitate a congress,
Soft as the morning bloom,
Redolent as the scent,
Of fresh honeysuckle,
And sweet as the nectar,
Dripping from the vine.

The passion of the kiss,
Seals the wedding sacrament,
And binds the pair,
Who spoke their vows,
And now share no more,
A mortal life alone.

Mae She Rest

Mae, the aunt, domestic, prim, and proper,
Sensible shoes, house dress, starched apron,
Downstairs servant girl,
Who married the chauffeur,
The figurine of bride and groom,
That graced their wedding cake,
Has rested fifty years upon a shelf,
Inside the cupboard.

Mae, the aunt of New Foundland stock,
Her maiden name, St. John,
A body like her native land,
Strong, tough, and oh so barren,
With the countenance and grace,
Of an anorectic turtle,
Thin lips, small hips,
Belly tucked inside a girdle.

Mae, the aunt, was healthy,
Not wealthy, but wise,
She canned fresh produce,
Cut down on fat,
Rationed cookies,
And candy and snacks...
Long before health foods,
Were fashionable.

To the children,
Of the neighborhood,
She was inscrutable,
Strict as a British constable.

Mae, the aunt, pious, righteous,
And to be avoided,
Daily prayed the rosary,
Weekly went to chapel,
She is from another time,
And won't adopt new customs,
She is wrapped in skin translucent,
Wrinkled, liver-spotted,
And prematurely ancient,
Smelling of ivory soap,
And lavender sachet,
Soft spoken, though her glare,
Could cut you like a scalpel.

Mae, the aunt, is legendary, dead,
But not forgotten,
Ramrod straight, no vice,
No under-lace.
Softened by Corn Huskers,
Made of ice,
Warmed occasionally,
By a toddy.

She was all virtue and virginity,
The Northern Lights,
Shown beneath her dress,
She didn't have a body.

In Peace

Mae, the aunt, had a secret chamber,
In her heart,
Capacious was her kindness,
I'd hear the family say.
She briefly raised the nieces,
That her sister couldn't always care,
Whose souls and mere existence,
Were in a state of disrepair.
Mae took it like a Spartan,
When she sent the girls away,
Hidden was her broken heart,
Her sadness and dismay.

Mae, the aunt, had a niece,
She cared for most,
And never even told her,
The girl of twelve,
She taught to read…
And loved,
But couldn't show it,

But Mae's caring was successful,
And the wounds were quick to heal,
Love has a way of getting through,
When feelings can't reveal,
She'd fed her tea and oranges,
Like Leonard Cohen recommended,
And once she kissed the niece,
Upon her cheek,
While sleeping,
She pretended.

Mae, the aunt, the niece,
For whom she cared,
She is my mother,
Whose own fierce devotion,
To her children,
Emulated Mae's – no other.

It wasn't that the aunt retired,
And the niece,
Lived happily-ever-after,
For Mae's work continued briefly,
With myself, and with my brother.
She'd feed me tea and oranges,
When I was hungry,
Stoned and wasted.
It was always,
Mae's kindness,

Not strong tea or bitter oranges,
That I tasted.

Mae, the aunt, she lived her final days,
In our home,
Being cared for by my mother,
Where silence reigned,
During many days,
Of awful pain and suffering,
When at last their history,
Drew their souls,
Into the cleansing fire,
Where hearts and tongues,
Ignite in words,
That speaks,
The heart's desire.

Mae the aunt, on her deathbed,
Is rumored this confession,
To have made:

"Patty, I should have told you,
That I loved you,
And didn't want,
To send you away"

The Wedding Anniversary
("Till Death Do Us part")

Wife

Our life,
You know,
Our time,
Upon,
This earth,
And,
All,
The,
Memories,
Are,
Mine now,
Now,
That,
You,
Are,
Gone.

Now,
That you,
Are gone,
I grieve,
Within,
The murky,

Hidden,
Places,
Buried,
Deep,
Within,
Me.

I have wept,
All,
The days,
Since,
You've,
Been gone,
Feeling,
All,
Alone…
One-
Hundred-
And,
Ninety-
Six,
Days,
It's been,
Since,
You,
Left me!

(The,
Longest,
That,
We've,
Ever,
Been,
Apart).

You know,
I didn't,
Hear,
The dirge,
Of,
Our dying,
Days,
It stole,
Upon me,
Like,
A,
Whimpering,
Banshee.
So,
I confused,
Her,
Lamentations,
With,
The gradual,
Quieting,

Of,
Your,
Labored,
Exhalations,
And suddenly -
It,
Seemed,

That,
Everything,
Over.

The Quiet...
A first time
Without,
Words,
To ,
Confirm,
Your,
Presence,
Without,
Language,
To,
Draw,
Us,
Close.

Other than,
The,
Wordless
Resonance,
Of
An,
Empty,
Room,
That,
Like,
A,
Cup,
Turned,
Upside,
Down,
Becomes,
My,
Small
Universe,
In,
Which,
Your,
Passing,
Spirit,
Might ,
Linger.

Were it real...
Would,
It,
Cause,
Ripples,
In,
The,
Delicate,
Fabric,
Of,
Diminished,
Space,
And,
Time,
Within,
Which,
I ,
Might,
Find,
Evidence,
Of
Your,
Existence?

If this should be,
My,
Universe,

Then,
I,
Will,
Put,
My,
Ear,
To,
The ,
Cup,
And,
Listen,
For,
Recorded,
Echoes,
Like,
Those,
Of,
Exploded,
Stars,
That,
Whisper,
Into,
SETI's,
Ears,
Erected,
In,
The,
Desert.

Heard,
First,
By,
The,
God,
Of,
The,
New,
Heaven,
And,
Now,
By,
Me,
As,
A,
Divine,
Gift...
To,
Be...
Granted!

I really did believe,
That,
We,
Would,
Always,
Be,
Together,
Because...,

We,
Always,
Were.

"Till Death Do US Part,"
Was,
A vow,
So sweet,
To me,

When,
I was,
Young,
And,
Joyful,
In,
The,
Communion,
That,
Joined,
Our,
Lives,
On,
May,
Eighth,
Nineteen-,
Forty-
Eight.

The future...Ah,
So,
Full,
Of,
Possibilities,
All,
Beginnings,
No,
Endings,
Like,
The,
Tonalities,
Of,
Sunlight,

In,
Springtime,
Lengthening ,
Into,
A,
Summer...
Without,
End!

I never anticipated,
That,
The,
Remnants,
Of,
Our,
Lives,
Were,
Meant,
To,
Keep,
In,
Silence,
Buried,
Under,
Earth,
Or,
Kept,
Upon,
A,
Mantle,
Above,
A,
Fireplace,
Filled,
With,
Cold,
Ashes.

It is still,
Only,
Silence,
That I...
Hear.

Husband

Don't you see me,
In,
The,
Album,
Of,
Memory?
Maybe,
When,
You,
Examine,
Old,
Photographs,
Or,
Are,
Visited,
By,
Recollections,
In,
The,
Day,
Or,

When,
You,
Walk,
With,
Me,
In,
Dreams,
At,
Night?

You talk to me,
Constantly,
In,
Your,
Prayers.
And,
I,
Hear,
Only,
Sorrow,
And,
Longing.

So,
Please,
Listen,
And,
Let me,
Speak,
To,
You...

Didn't you,
Hear,
Me,
Say,
Goodbye,
And,
That ,
I,
Loved,
You,
When,
I died?

I,
Could,
Not,
Move,
My.
Lips,
Or,
Voice,
The,
Words,

But,
I,
Know,
It,
Echoed,
In,
The,
Soughing,
Of,
The,
Wind,
And,
The,
Ticking,
Of,
The,
Clock,

Hung,
In,
The,
Parlor,

You must,
Have,
Heard,
It,
In,
The,
Chirping,
Of,
The,
Crickets,
And,
In,
The,
Laughter,
Of,
Our,
Grandchildren,
In,
The,
Days,
That,
Followed.

I tried,
To,
Talk,
To,
You,
Through,
The,
Daily,
Rhythms,
Of,
Your,
Life.

But,
The,
Heavy,
Pounding,
That,
Was,
The,
Beating,
Of,
Your,
 heart,
Always,
Drowned,
Me,
Out.

You don't know this,
But,
On,
The,
Afternoon,
I died,
I ,
Saw,
You,
And,
All,
Our,
Children,
At,
My,
Bedside,
And,
You,
Shone,
Brightly,
Even,
Though,
My,
Eyes,
Grew
Dull,

Even,
As,
 I,
Began,
To,
Slip,
Away.

(And I was,
So,
Moved,
By,
All,
Of,
This,
Wonderful…
Strangeness.)

I wanted to take you,
With,
Me,
Somewhere,
Somewhere,
Familiar,
And,
Beautiful,

And,
I,
Wanted,
To,
Offer,
You,
Something.

Something,
Like,
The,
Prospect,
Of,
Starting,
Over,
Of
A,
New,
Love,
Or,
Just,
Give,
You,
A color,
Postcard,

Of,
An,
Indescribable,
Heaven,
Glimpsed,
Only,
Briefly.

I wanted you,
To,
Listen,
To,
Me,
As if,
You,
Were,
Hearing,
An,
Original,
Recording,
Of,
Our,
Favorite,
Songs,

Like,
The,
Ones,
You,
Used,
To,
Sing.

I wish,
That,
I,
Could,
Reach,
Out,
And,
Pull,
Off,
The,
Veil,
Of,
Grief,
That,
Darkens,
Your,
Days,

And,
Blends,
Them,
With,
The,
Night.

I wish,
That,
 I could,
Do,
It,
Like,
A ,
Parlor,
Trick.

Snatch,
It,
Away,
Like,
A,
Black,
Cloth,
From,
A,
Table,
Setting,

Leaving,
Fine,
China,
And,
Polished,
Silver,
Undisturbed....
Like,
Beautiful,
Memories,
Left,
Upon,
The,
Table.
Inviting,
The,
Living,
To,
Feast,
Upon,
A,
Life...

So,
Beautiful,
Bountiful,
And,
Rare…

As…
We
Once,
Had.

Reprised from a poem written May, 1997
following the death of the poet's   father.

Babble

I am a man of words,
Always thinking of,
What next to say.
If I say, that I know myself,
And that I *am,*
Then, therefore,
I do exist,
That is…
In the sense that,
I think I do….
Right?

I am confirmed,
By the language,
Spoken in my head,
In English no less,
So it would seem,
That I exist,
Even during,
My quiet moments.

And when,
In the presence,
Of other English thinkers,
That is,
When in their company,
I exist,
For them as well,
And, Oh …,
Me too,
Right?

If I gesture,
To a foreigner,
Who speaks, say,
Limbu,
Do I communicate,
More than just,
An up-raised palm,
Which signifies,
(In my way of thinking):
"I come in peace,"
Or, just…
Hi!

To him,
I may have *said,*
"Fuck you…,
Let's get it on."

How does,
"I think,
Therefore, I am,"
Translate,
In Limbu?

Speaking….
Is no more permanent,
Than thinking words,
More lasting is writing,
Although not universal,
It's more explicit,
In meaning,
When read by,
A literate fellow.

Developed over the millennia,
The written word,
Has changed,
Slowly over time,
Such that,
Those who speak,
Colloquially,
Are mystified,
And unaware.
That,
Subtle changes,
Have occurred.

If I should write,
The written words,
That other's read,
I'd better watch my spelling,
If I write *reed*,
Instead of *read,*
Will they,
Fetch Egyptian papyrus,
Or pick up,
What I've written,
And,
Read it?

I will especially,
Avoid *speaking,*
In transient, non-linear,
Latin alphabetical,
Adaptations,
In other words,
No.....
Morse code,
Sign language,
Semaphore flag waving,
Or smoke signals.

I'll be careful when I write,
Not to lean my "R"s,
In cursive,
Because of confusions,
Caused by,
All the allographs,
Of a grapheme,
Such as when writing
Is cursive,
Block letters,
Or type…
Oh, my!

And don't confuse,
The letters,
Even more so,
By mixing up,
The majuscule, and miniscule;
The upper cases,
And lower cases,
Of the 26-letters,
Of the alphabet,
And don't use all of one,
Or all of the other,
And damn it!
Don't use hearts and circles,
When dotting the "Is,"
In your love letters.

I'll be careful,
When I speak,
Not to roll my "Rs,"
Unless I'm speaking,
Spanish,
Should my tripping words,
Be misconstrued,
By others,
Who think I have,
A speech impediment.

We should all study writing,
At Lascaux Cave University,
Learning from,
The logographs,
 Painted on the walls,
In other words,
The drawings made,
By cave men,
Who told it,
Like it was,
(If it looks like a mastodon,
It is a mastodon,
Or was),
That form,
Doesn't ever change.

Pictographic, Ideographic,
Stick figures Rule!

 Please don't chew gum,
When speaking,
And stay put,
In New Jersey.

Dialects are only cute,
When you speak,
The language,
You have learned,
While being raised,
By Canadian geese,
Or Italian wolves,
Like Romulus,
And Remus.

So stay with,
Your flock.
Or your pack.

And god forbid!
Do not speak,
The Olde,
Queen's English here,
For we ridded it once,
From American shores,
When we chased the Brits,
With musket,
And canon,
And purged our language,
Of their pompous,
Supercilious,
Affectations.

We signed,
Quite clearly,
With up-raised fist,
And middle finger extended,
No confusion ever intended,
That to the Imperial crown,
It said...
Fuck it!

I don't know any better,
Who I am,
For thinking,
That *I am*,
Because I thought it.
I know,
That I am prejudiced,
And prone to making judgments,
I corner myself often,
Because my reasoning,
Like an acrostic,
That's been written,
In genetic code,
Has got me thinking,
Left-to-right,
And up-side down,
And sideways.

Like running into yourself,
Going this way,
And that,
And meeting yourself,
Coming and going.

We have all,
Been afflicted,
By the boustro-
Phendonic,
Associated with,
Directionality,
In writing,
Reading,
And thinking.

We are what we learn,
And learning,
The language,
Of our kin,
Makes us,
Limited,
Contextual,
Narrow-minded,
And dumb.

A dog chasing his tail,
Is showing us,
Through ritual and dance,
The harm,
That circumlocution,
Convoluted thinking,
And read'n and writ'n,
Can do!

I wag my tail,
And dance...
Therefore, I am!

- For our edification, I've included a list of languages upon which our babble is built.

Language index

An alphabetical index of all the languages featured on Omniglot.

A | B | C | D | E | F | G | H | I | J | K | L | M | N | O | P | Q | R | S | T | U | V | W | X | Y | Z |

What is writing? | Abjads | Alphabets | Syllabic Alphabets | Syllabaries | Semanto-phonetic scripts | Undeciphered scripts | Alternative scripts | Your con-scripts | Writing direction index | Languages by writing system | A-Z index | Site map | Search this site |

A Abaza | Abenaki | Abkhaz | Adyghe | Afaan Oromo | Afar | Afrikaans | Aghul | Ahom | Ainu | Akan | Akhvakh | Alabama | Albanian | Aleut | Alsatian | Altay | Amarakaeri | Amharic | Amis | Anglo-Saxon | Anutan | Apache | Arabela | Arabic | Arabic (Egyptian) | Arabic (Lebanese) | Arabic (Syrian) | Aragonese | Aramaic | Aranese | Arapaho | Archi | Armenian | Aromanian | Arrernte | Arvanitic | Assamese | Asturian | Atayal, Avar | Avestan | Aymara | Azeri |

B Bagatha | Balinese | Balkar | Baluchi | Bambara | Baniwa | Bashkir | Basque | Bassa | Batak | Belarusian | Bemba | Bengali | Bhojpuri | Bikol | Bislama | Blackfoot | Bora | Bosnian | Breton | Bugis | Buhid | Bulgarian | Burmese | Burushaski | Buryat | Bhutanese |

C Cantonese | Cape Verdean Creole | Carrier | Catalan | Cayuga | Cebuano | Celtiberian | Cham | Chamorro | Chavacano | Chechen | Cherokee | Cheyenne | Chichewa | Chickasaw | Chinese | Choctaw | Chukchi | Chuvash | Cimbrian | Cofán | Comanche | Coptic | Cornish | Corsican | Cree | Creek | Crimean Tatar | Croatian | Cypriot | Cyrillic | Czech |

D Danish | Dargwa | Dari | Dawan | Dehong Dai | Delaware | Dhivehi | Dholuo | Dinka | Dong | Drehu | Duala | Dungan | Dutch | Dzongkha (Bhutanese) |

E English | Erzya | Esperanto | Estonian | Etruscan | Even | Evenki | Ewe | Ewondo | Eyak |

91

F Faroese | Fijian | Filipino | Finnish | Folkspraak | French | Frisian | Friulian |

G Ga | Gadaba | Gagauz | Galician | Gan | Ganda | Garo | Ge'ez | Genoese | Georgian | German | Gondi | Gooniyandi | Gothic | Goudu | Greek | Greenlandic | Guadeloupean Creole | Guarani | Gugadja/Kukatja | Gujarati | Gwich'in |
H Haida | Haitian Creole | Hakka | Hän | Hanuno'o | Hausa | Hawaiian | Hebrew | Herero | Hiligaynon | Hindi | Hixkaryana | Hmong | Ho | Hopi | Hotcąk | Hsihsia | Hungarian | Huasteco |
I Iberian | Icelandic | Ido | Igbo | Ilocano | Indonesian | Ingush | Interglossa | Interlingua | Inuktitut | Iñupiaq | Irish | Italian |
J Jamaican | Japanese | Jatapu | Javanese | Jèrriais (Jersey Norman French) | Judeo-Arabic |

K Kabardian | Kabyle | Kaingang | Kala Lagaw Ya | Kalmyk | Kammara | Kannada | Kanuri | Kapampangan | Kaqchikel | Karakalpak | Karamojong | Karelian | Kashmiri | Kashubian | Kayah Li | Kazakh | Kazakh | Kekchi | Ket | Khanty | Khitan | Khmer | Kinyarwanda | Kildin Sami | Kiribati | Kirundi | Klallam | Klamath | Koasati | Kolam | Komi | Konda-Dora | Konkani | Korean | Koryak | Kotia | Kpelle | Kumyk | Kupia | Kurdish | Kwakiutl | Kyrghyz |
L Ladino | Lak | Lanna | Lao | Latin | Latvian | Laz | Lepcha | Lezgi | Lingua Franca Nova | Limbu | Lingala | Lithuanian | Livonian | Lojban | Loma | Lombard | Low Saxon | Latino sine Flexione | Luxembourgish | Lycian | Lydian |
M Maasai | Macedonian | Maithili | Makassarese | Makhuwa | Malachim | Malagasy | Malay | Malayalam | Mali | Maltese | Maldivian | Mam | Manchu | Mandaic | Mandarin Chinese | Mandekan | Manipuri | Mansi | Manx | Māori | Marathi | Mari | Marshallese | Massachusett | Mayan | Mende | Meriam Mir | Meroïtic | Miami | Mikasuki | Mi'kmaq | Mingrelian | Mirandese | Modi | Mohawk | Moksha | Moldovan | Mongolian | Montagnais |

Moriori | Mukha Dora | Mundari | Murrinh-Patha | Murui Huitoto |
N Nabataean | Nagamese | Nahuatl | Nama | Nanai | Naskapi | Navajo | Naxi | Ndebele | Ndjuká | Neapolitan | Nenets | Nepali | Ngiyambaa | Nheengatu | Niuean | N☐uu | Nivkh | Noongar | Norn, Norwegian | Novial | Northern Sotho | Northern Thai (Kam Mu'ang) | Nuer, Nushu | Nuu-Chah-Nulth (Nootka) | N☐uu |
O Occidental | Occitan | Ojibwe | Okinawan | Old Church Slavonic | Old English | Old Norse | Oneida | O'odham | Oriya | Orkhon | Oshi Wambo | Ossetian | Otomi |
P Pali | Papiamento | Parthian | Pashto | Persian (Farsi) | Phoenician | Piedmontese | Pipil | Pirahã | Pitjantjatjara | Polish | Pomo (Eastern) | Porja | Portuguese | Potawatomi | Punjabi
Q Q'eqchi' | Quechua | Quenya |

R Rana | Ranjana | Rarotongan | Redjang | Romanian | Romansh | Romany | Rotokas | Rotuman | Russian | Ruthenian |
S Saami/Sami | Saanich | Sabaean | Sakao | Samaritan | Samoan | Sango | Sanskrit | Santali | Saramaccan | Sardinian | Savara | Scots | Scottish Gaelic | Serbian | Seri | Seychelles Creole | Southern Sotho | Shabaki | Shan | Shanghainese | Sharda | Shavante | Shawnee | Shilluk | Shona | Shoshone | Sicilian | Siddham | Silesian | Sindhi | Sinhala | Sioux | Siraiki | Slovak | Slovene | Slovio | Sogdian | Solresol | Somali | Sora | Sorbian | Sourashtra | Spanish | Sranan | Sugali | Sundanese | Svan | Swahili | Swati/Swazi | Swedish | Sylheti | Syriac |
T Tabassaran | Tagalog | Tagbanwa | Tahitian | Tai Dam | Tai Lue | Taiwanese | Tajik | Tamajaq | Tamasheq | Tamil | Tatar | Teochew | Telugu | Tetum | Thai | Theban | Tibetan | Tamazight | Tigrinya | Tlingit | Tocharian | Tok Pisin | Tokelauan | Tongan | Tsez | Tshiluba | Tsonga | Tsotsil | Tswana | Tuareg | Tucano | Tumbuka | Turkish | Turkmen | Tuscarora | Tuvaluan | Tuvan | Twi |
U Ubykh | Udmurt | Ugaritic | Ukrainian | Urdu | Uyghur | Uzbek |

V Vai | Venda | Venetian | Vietnamese | Volapük | Võro | Votic |

W Wakhi | Walloon | Waray-Waray | Warlpiri | Wayuu | Welsh | Wik-Mungkan | Wiradjuri | Wolof |
X Xavante | Xhosa | Xiang | Xixia |

Y Yakut | Yapese | Yaqui | Yerukula | Yi | Yiddish | Yindjibarndi | Yolngu | Yoruba | Yukaghir | Yupik | Yurok |
Z Záparo | Zapotec | Zarma | Zazaki | Zhuang | Zulu | Zuni |

www.ingramcontent.com/pod-product-compliance
Lightning Source LLC
Chambersburg PA
CBHW032020040426
42448CB00006B/681